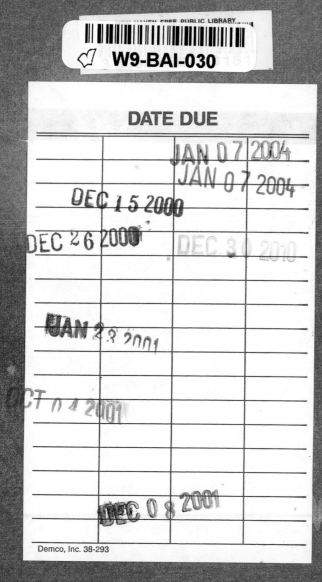

Copyright © 1999 by Nord-Süd Verlag AG, Gossau Zürich, Switzerland
First published in Switzerland under the title *Stille Nacht, heilige Nacht.*
Introduction translation copyright © 1999 by North-South Books Inc.

First published in the United States, Great Britain, Canada,
Australia, and New Zealand in 1999 by North-South Books,
an imprint of Nord-Süd Verlag AG, Gossau Zürich, Switzerland.

Distributed in the United States by North-South Books Inc., New York.

Library of Congress Cataloging-in-Publication Data is available.
A CIP catalogue record for this book is available from The British Library.
ISBN 0-7358-1152-0 (trade binding)
1 3 5 7 9 TB 10 8 6 4 2
ISBN 0-7358-1153-9 (library binding)
1 3 5 7 9 LB 10 8 6 4 2
Printed in Belgium

For more information about our books, and the authors and artists
who create them, visit our web site: http://www.northsouth.com

Silent Night, Holy Night

A Christmas Carol by Joseph Mohr

Illustrated by Maja Dusíková

North-South Books · New York · London

THE STORY OF SILENT NIGHT

IT WAS CHRISTMAS EVE and the town of Oberndorf, Austria, was blanketed in snow. The houses and trees were covered in a mantle of white and even the steeple of St. Nicholas church wore a snowcap.

Inside the church everything was ready for midnight mass. The big Christmas tree was decorated. A Nativity scene was set up. As the choir members gathered for rehearsal that afternoon, the church was filled with their joy and anticipation. But when the organist, Franz Gruber, sat down at the organ to accompany them, no note sounded.

Legend has it that a little mouse was the cause. Unable to find a crumb of bread in the squeaky-clean church, it had nibbled a hole in the organ bellows.

What is known for certain is that the organ *was* broken, and Father Joseph Mohr, the priest who would be saying midnight mass that Christmas Eve, was concerned. How could they celebrate without music? He decided to write the lyrics for a little song. Then he asked Franz Gruber to set the words to music. The organist scribbled a simple melody and the two rehearsed together, with Father Mohr accompanying them on his guitar.

That night, Christmas Eve 1818, at the midnight mass at St. Nicholas church in Oberndorf, Austria, they sang the new song. And so "Silent Night," one of the world's best-known and best-loved Christmas carols, was born.

MAJA DUSÍKOVÁ

Silent night,
   holy night,

All is calm,

all is bright.

*Round yon Virgin
Mother and Child,
Holy Infant
so tender and mild,
Sleep in heavenly peace;
Sleep in heavenly peace.*

Silent night,
  holy night,

Shepherds quake at the sight.
Glories stream from heaven afar,
Heav'nly hosts sing
Alleluia.

Christ the Saviour is born;
  Christ the Saviour is born.

Silent night,
holy night,

Son of God,
love's pure light.
Radiant beams
from Thy holy face,
With the dawn
of redeeming grace,

Jesus, Lord, at Thy birth,
   Jesus, Lord, at Thy birth.